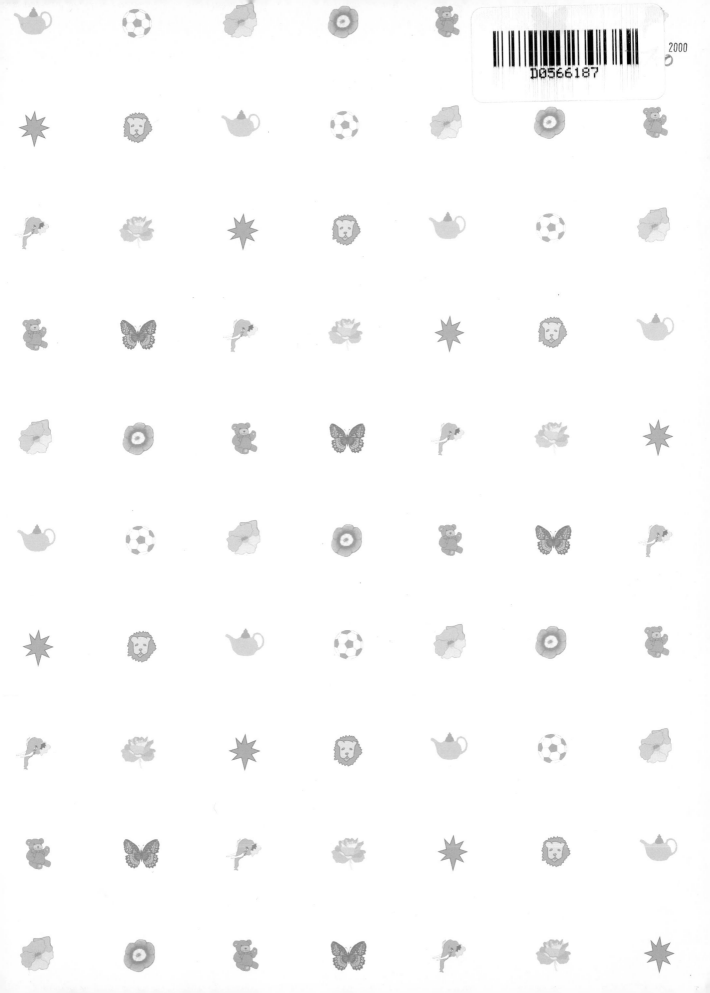

3-D Découpage
made easy

3-D Découpage
made easy

Series Editors: Susan & Martin Penny

David & Charles

A DAVID & CHARLES BOOK

First published in the UK in 1999

A catalogue record for this book is available from the British Library.

ISBN 0 7153 0931 5

Series Editors: Susan & Martin Penny
Designed and produced by Penny & Penny
Illustrations: Fred Fieber at Red Crayola
Photography: Jon Stone

Printed in Italy by L.E.G.O. S.p.A.
for David & Charles
Brunel House Newton Abbot Devon

Contents

Introduction to 3-D Découpage

3-D Découpage Made Easy is a complete guide to the craft of 3-D découpage; this enjoyable and relaxing hobby allows you to produce pictures with physical depth and interest, from a set of identical prints of the same design. These can be found on giftwrap, wallpaper and fabric; produced on a photocopier, stamped or cut from card

Essential equipment

Below is a list of equipment needed for 3-D découpage:

- **Scissors** – used for cutting out the layers of a design.
- **Craft knife and cutting mat** – used for cutting intricate detail.
- **Tweezers** – used for positioning the paper pieces on to silicone blobs.
- **Cocktail stick** – used for nudging the paper pieces into position.
- **Small coin** – used to check the distance between the layers is the same.
- **Barbecue skewer** – used for making a bridge on the back of narrow paper pieces.
- **Thin florist's wire** – used to strengthen very narrow pieces of paper.
- **Spray adhesive** – for attaching the base layer of the picture.
- **Newspaper** – used for covering your work surface when using spray adhesive.
- **PVA or white craft glue** – used for gluing parts of the design together.
- **Felt-tipped pens** – for colouring the cut edges of coloured paper pieces.
- **Soft pencil** – for colouring the cut edges of light-coloured paper pieces.
- **Shaping tool and mat or spoon** – for shaping the top layer of the picture.
- **Ruler** – used as a guide when cutting straight lines.
- **Paintbrush** – for applying watercolour paints.

What to use ?

Below is a list of items that may be a good source for 3-D découpage:

- **Giftwrap** – use good quality paper with multiple images and well defined edges.
- **Wallpaper** – images must stand out well from the background and be close together.

- **Fabric** – use lightweight furnishing fabric with a tight weave, close pattern repeat and strong single images.
- **Colour photocopies** – use the stiffest paper that will work in the photocopier.
- **Stamps** – choose stamps with good clear images and plenty of space for colouring.
- **Photographs** – choose your subject with care: landscapes with well defined edges work best. Use matt prints and colour the cut edges.
- **Watercolour paper** – use the thinnest paper, available, which can be painted, cut out and then assembled.
- **Coloured or crinkle paper and card** – 3-D découpage does not have to be restricted to pre-printed images. Use plain paper or card to make simple pictures.

Useful hints and tips

✔ Attach the base layer using spray adhesive

✔ Always apply silicone using a cocktail stick

✔ Position the paper pieces using tweezers

✔ Never press down on the paper pieces being attached or the silicone will spread

✔ Use a small coin to check that the layers are the same distance apart

✔ Cut the paper using small sharp scissors and the intricate detail using a craft knife

✔ Colour the cut edges of the paper pieces

✔ Varnish will protect the paper from dust

✔ Overcut a piece if it will be partially hidden behind a subsequent layers

Special effects

✔ Use feathering on the edge of birds' feathers

✔ Cut animal fur using the furring technique

✔ Add highlights to the top layer of a picture using nail varnish

✔ If you have a paper piece that is narrow and difficult to position, make a wooden bridge to support it from a cocktail stick or barbecue skewer

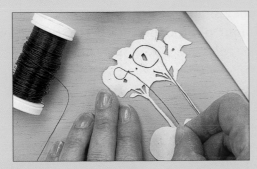

✔ If the piece is very narrow, like a flower stem, make a bridge from fine wire

✔ Build another scene behind a window or door for a greater feeling of distance

✔ Add shape to the top layer of a picture, by making the paper concave or convexed using a special tool or spoon

How to display your work?

Here are some useful tips for helping you choose the right way to display your 3-D découpage.

● **Pictures**

Use a recessed frame

A mount can be used in front of the picture or in between the layers

Attach the base layer to a backing board using spray adhesive

Use handmade paper behind the design for an interesting effect

Attach the layers on silicone blobs or sticky pads

Glass will keep the picture dust free

● **Greetings cards**

Use ready-made card blanks or make your own from thin card

Silicone blobs will give a stronger finish

If you want to put the card into an envelope, use just a few layers, or build the layers on tabs that can be flattened

● **Baubles**

Clear plastic with a flat circular surface for applying the base layer

Comes in several different sizes

Use silicone blobs or sticky pads

Both sides of the dome can be used

● **Gift tags**

Use ready-made tags or make your own from card

Parcel labels are cheap and very strong

Silicone blobs will give a stronger finish

● **Lampshades**

Should be made from paper or fabric-covered paper

Must have a flat surface

Attach the layers using silicone

● **Gift holders**

Use ready-made paper gift bags or boxes

Make your own bags from gift paper or wallpaper, and boxes from stiff card

● **Boxes**

Use cardboard or wooden boxes

Can be painted to match the design

The 3-D layers can be displayed on the top or sides of the box

Planning and Cutting

Perspective is the most important part of creating a three-dimensional picture. Remember to plan and construct the picture from the base layer: this means the things in the foreground will be the last items to be positioned. When a subject extends behind a subsequent layer, it should be cut larger to avoid the edges being seen

Planning your 3-D

Look at the picture and decide what is in the back, middle and front. Cut out a complete picture: this is the base layer. Then cut out the other layers, working from the back.

Cutting with scissors

Cut around shapes with small sharp scissors. Use the middle of the scissors, turning the scissors not the paper. Avoid cutting curves as a series of straight lines.

Cutting with a knife

1 Use a craft knife and cutting mat to cut intricate detail. The knife should have a straight sharp pointed blade and you should change the blade if it starts to pull on the paper. Make definite cuts in the paper, following the outlines.

2 If the cut does not go right through the paper, cut the line again. Do not pull the pieces apart or you will be left with a ragged edge and the picture will be ruined.

Overcutting

When cutting layers that will be partially hidden behind subsequent layers, cut the design larger, and include a small amount of the overlapping subject. When the upper layer is positioned on top, the cut edge of the lower subject will be well hidden under the upper layer.

Receding background

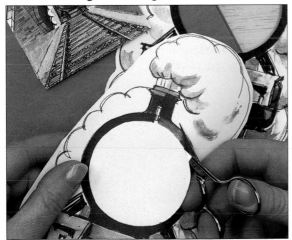

On some subjects you can achieve a greater feeling of distance by building another scene behind the main picture. This can be done where there is a window or doorway; or like the train on page 52 where the scene continues behind the main picture. Always make sure you overcut the parts to be receded.

Feathering

Holding the scissors in one hand, turn your wrists inward, tilting the heels of both thumbs downward and towards each other. This will lay the scissor blades at an acute angle almost touching the paper. As you cut the paper will curl: the finer the cuts, the more realistic the feathers will look.

Furring

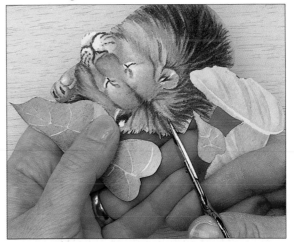

In furring the cut paper should have square edges not round, and very little curl. First, cut away the areas of paper that are not part of the design then, holding the scissors at right angles to the paper, make short straight cuts of varying lengths. This will give the appearance of realistic looking animal fur.

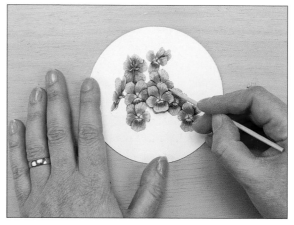

Building a Picture

When building a three-dimensional picture line up the layers exactly, with no more than a shadow of the underneath piece showing. Use blobs of silicone or self-adhesive sticky pads to space the layers apart, taking care not to get them too close, or to give them too much height, so losing the perspective and realism of the picture

Building layers

1 Silicone rubber adhesive is very similar to the sealant used around baths and wash basins. It dries almost clear and does not run or shrink. Use the end of a cocktail stick to apply 5mm (¼in) blobs to the base layer, not to the paper piece you are adding.

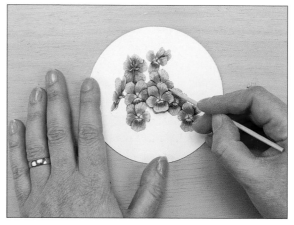

3 Use a cocktail stick to nudge the paper piece gently into position; try to get the piece exactly over the shape underneath. The silicone will take about half an hour to dry completely, so you will have ample time to adjust the position.

2 Position the paper piece on to the silicone blob using tweezers; do not press the paper down, or you will flatten the picture and the silicone will spread.

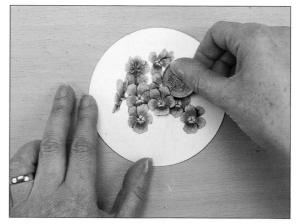

4 Try to get the right height between layers – too little will not look three-dimensional and too much will make the pieces float. A gap the thickness of a coin is a good guide.

Self-adhesive pads

For pictures cut from card, or to make it easier for children to enjoy 3-D découpage, self-adhesive sticky pads can be used to build up the layers. Cut the pads into small pieces, peel off the backing paper on one side, then press the pad in position. Remove the top protective paper before adding the next layer.

Wooden bridge

If you have a paper piece that is narrow and difficult to position, it will help to support the area before attaching it. Glue a wooden bridge, cut from a cocktail stick or barbecue skewer on to the back, then you will need fewer blobs of silicone, which can be positioned where they will not show.

Paper tabs

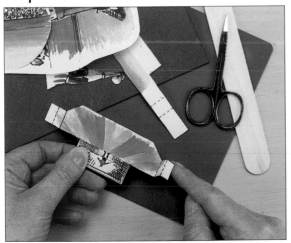

Tabs are only suitable for a picture where they will be hidden behind another layer. Extend the paper pieces at the edges by drawing and cutting tabs; when scored, folded and positioned the tabs will give the pieces enough height to form a bridge over the previous layer.

Wire supports

Use this technique when you have a very thin piece of paper to support, like a flower stem. Bend a length of thin wire into the shape of the stem, looping it at the top and bottom for added strength. Apply white tacky glue to the back of the paper and press the wire firmly in position.

Finishing Techniques

These extra special finishing touches will give your projects a more professional look: shaping the top layer of the design, particularly on floral subjects, will give it depth and interest; cut edges can be coloured to stop them showing; and a coat of varnish will seal the finished picture and keep it free from dust

Shaping and curving

Shape the top layer by laying it on a mat, and rubbing with a shaping tool or spoon. The side of the paper you work on will depend on how you want the paper to curve.

Varnishing

Your finished picture can be varnished using a paper varnish; or small areas can be coated with clear nail varnish. Apply the varnish thinly, in small areas, building up the coats.

Colouring edges

All the edges of the pieces should be shaded to hide the white cut paper. Use toning felt-tipped pens on coloured paper, and a soft pencil if the subject has a sketched outline.

Mounting

A recessed frame is needed to display your finished picture. This can be made to size or bought ready-made from craft suppliers. Glass will protect the picture from dust.

Sourcing Different Images

As well as pictures specially printed for 3-D use, you can source printed images from elsewhere: wallpaper and giftwrap can be used if printed with a repeat pattern. Use good quality paper; thin paper may curl up when cut. Multiple images can also be produced using a rubber stamp, which are coloured after stamping

Using stamps

Choose stamps with good clear images and plenty of space for adding colour. Stamp multiple images, then colour using felt-tipped pens, before cutting out the layers.

Using wallpaper

Use wallpaper or borders where the images that you will be using stand out well against the background and close together, or you will need lots of the paper.

Using fabric

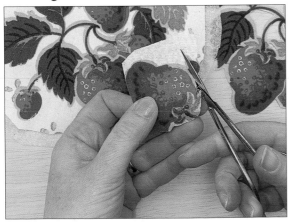

Use lightweight furnishing fabric with a tight weave, close pattern repeat and strong single images. Iron interfacing on to the back before cutting the fabric.

Using giftwrap

Wrapping paper is readily available, and if chosen carefully can make a good subject for 3-D work. Use good quality paper with multiple images and well defined edges.

Botanical Picture

Create a botanical style picture and pretty gift box and tag using floral giftwrap. Use paper with clear images and well defined edges to make cutting easier. When shaped and layered the flowers look like specimens torn from the pages of a botanical notebook

Choose giftwrap that has at least six copies of the same illustration, or buy several sheets of the same paper.

You will need

- Floral giftwrap with repeat design and border
- Silicone glue
- Wooden box frame
- Thick card – cream
- Craft knife, cutting mat, scissors
- Fine sandpaper
- Acrylic paint – red
- Handmade or textured paper
- Paper glue or spray adhesive, blunt knife
- 3-D découpage shaping mat and tool, or spoon
- Double-sided sticky tape
- Hole punch

Building layers

1 Silicone is a clear glue-like substance that is used to hold the layers of the picture in position. You can also build the layers using self-adhesive sticky pads, but for a small detailed design like the flowers opposite, silicone is more flexible.

2 Although the silicone container has a fine nozzle and can be used straight from the tube, it is much easier to apply using a cocktail stick. Apply blobs of silicone between 2mm ($^1/_{16}$in) and 5mm ($^1/_4$in) high on to the fixed layer, not to the back of the paper piece being applied; position a blob roughly in the centre, and if needed smaller blobs closer to the edges. Keep the silicone well away from the outer edges of the paper or it will show in your finished picture, and avoid getting it on your fingers as this will make handling the paper pieces very difficult. Do not start applying the silicone until you have cut the next paper layer, or it may dry before you can apply the paper.

3 Use tweezers to position the paper pieces on to the silicone, and a cocktail stick to nudge the paper gently into position. Do not press hard on the paper pieces, as it may spread the silicone and flatten the layers beneath. Make sure that each piece is directly over the picture beneath: this is important as the overall effect will be spoiled if the layers are not in line.

Preparing the frame

1 Lightly sand the box frame, then wipe over with a damp cloth to remove any dust. Pick up a little red acrylic paint on to a paintbrush and then drag the paint around the frame working in one direction. Leave to dry.

2 Check that the giftwrap border will fit into the frame; if it is too large you will need to shorten each side when you cut it out. Tear a rectangle of textured paper 6mm (¼in) wider on all sides than the border. To do this, tear the paper against a ruler.

3 Remove the board back from the frame; stick a layer of cream paper over the board, and then the torn paper centrally on top using glue or spray adhesive.

Cutting out the border

1 On a cutting mat and using a sharp craft knife, cut the border from the giftwrap. Make sure your craft knife blade is very sharp; if you use a blunt blade you may damage the print. You can also use small embroidery scissors for cutting the larger shapes.

2 Using glue or spray adhesive, attach the border to the background paper: this is the base layer.

3 Cut out the second border layer, exactly the same as the base layer. Position it over the base layer on small blobs of silicone. When cutting the layers remove any detail areas between the leaves, before removing the main background area: this will make the paper easier to handle.

4 Cut individual leaves or fruit from the border for the third layer, then attach them to the second layer using very small blobs of silicone.

Cutting the flowers

1 Cut the flower cluster, stalk and leaves in one piece: this is the base layer. If the design has a shadow, do not cut it as part of the design. Secure the base layer on to the centre of the textured paper using glue or spray adhesive.

2 Cut the second layer the same as the base layer, including all parts of the design. Apply blobs of silicone on to the base layer, then position the second layer on top making sure it is positioned exactly over the base layer.

3 To give the design depth you will need about another five layers. Cut out the flower cluster, omitting several flower heads: each time you omit part of the design it will recede into the background. Fix the third layer in place using silicone.

4 On subsequent layers omit more flower heads. For the last few layers, use single flower heads, building up the height on some more than others (see the step-by-step diagrams on the following page). Before attaching the last layer, shape the petals to

Cutting the flowers

1 Cut the complete flower for the base and second layer.

2 For the third layer, cut the flower cluster from the paper, then carefully remove the flower heads that are furthest away.

3 For the fourth layer, cut away more heads, taking care that the areas between the flowers are the same on all layers.

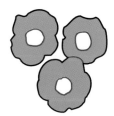

4 For the fifth and subsequent layers, keep reducing the number of heads until you are cutting individual flowers.

give them life and form, using a shaping tool, or spoon. To do this, lay the paper face up on a shaping pad or cutting mat and then using a shaping tool or spoon handle, gently rub the paper in a circular movement following the shape of the petals to give them a concave appearance (see Finishing Techniques, page 12). Do not press too hard or the paper will crease. Fix the final layer in place using silicone.

Cutting the leaves

1 The base and first layer of the leaves are already in position, so now is the time to decide how to position the subsequent layers. Cut out the leaves in one piece, then study their positions: some will be further back than others. Cut away the leaves that are furthest away, then fix the layer in place using silicone.

2 Repeat the process, removing the leaves that are furthest back as you cut each layer. The final layer should be single leaves, shaping the edges to give them form in the same way as the flowers. Build up the layers of leaves to the same level as the flower head.

Assembling the picture

1 When the silicone is dry, assemble the picture in the frame. Replace the glass as this will help to protect the picture from dust and dirt.

Making the gift box

1 Following the measurements on page 19, draw a box shape on to thin card. Cut out the shape following the solid lines.

2 Score along the broken lines with the back of a blunt knife and then fold backwards along the scored lines, forming the box shape. Open out the box and lay it on a flat surface.

Cutting the flowers

1 Cut out the base layer of the flowers and leaves and stick it centrally on the box front using glue or spray adhesive.

2 Cut out a second layer, exactly the same as the base layer, then carefully attach it to the base using blobs of silicone.

3 Build up the layers, removing petals in the same way as you did for the picture. You will need at least another five layers, omitting more petals on each layer.

4 The stalk, bud and leaves should only have two or three layers as they are behind the main flower heads.

5 On the top layers curl the individual petals under at the tips using the shaping tool or spoon (see Finishing Techniques, page 10); attach the petals to the box.

Assembling the box

1 To assemble the box: re-fold along the scored lines, then use double-sided sticky tape to attach the tabs to the base and sides.

Making the tag

1 Make a tracing of the template opposite, and cut a gift tag from card, then using a punch, make a hole at the top. Cut out two small flower heads from the giftwrap, then découpage them on to the tag. Thread the tag with a length of ribbon.

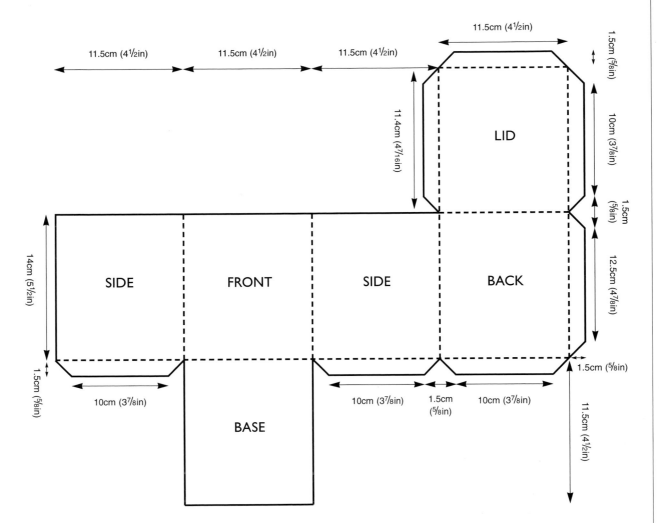

11.5cm (4½in)   11.5cm (4½in)   11.5cm (4½in)   11.5cm (4½in)

1.5cm (⅝in)

10cm (3⅞in)

LID

11.4cm (4⁷⁄₁₆in)

1.5cm (⅝in)

14cm (5½in)

SIDE   FRONT   SIDE   BACK

12.5cm (4⅞in)

1.5cm (⅝in)

10cm (3⅞in)   10cm (3⅞in)   1.5cm (⅝in)   10cm (3⅞in)

1.5cm (⅝in)

11.5cm (4½in)

BASE

Use the measurements above to
make your own gift box.

Use this template to cut a gift tag
from thick card. Punch a hole at
the top and thread with ribbon.

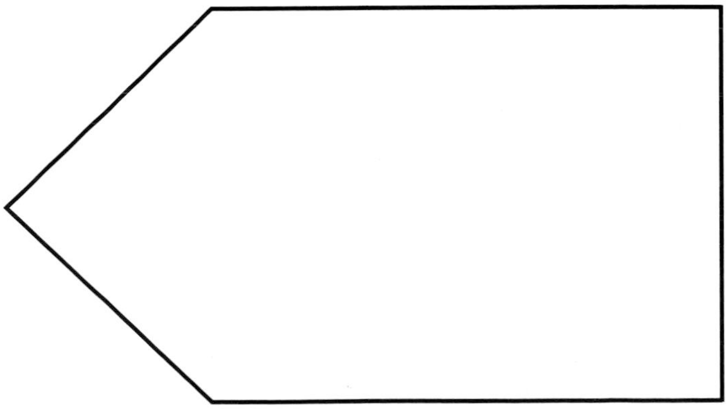

Christmas Baubles

These delightful Christmas baubles are made from photocopies of original chalk pastel illustrations given with this project. Each picture is built using at least four layers, making the finished bauble very three-dimensional. Use them to decorate a holly wreath or to bring new life to your Christmas tree

If you are unable to buy the baubles, these designs can also be used to decorate Christmas cards. Cut them out in the same way as for the baubles, then assemble the layers on the front of a card blank.

You will need
- Domed clear plastic baubles 80mm – available from most good craft shops
- Colour photocopy of the illustrations (pages 23-25)
- Scissors, craft knife, cutting mat
- Silicone glue
- Spray adhesive or double-sided sticky tape
- Tweezers, cocktail stick

Copying and cutting

1 On pages 23-25 you will find six identical illustrations of three different designs: a village scene, robin and teddy. Colour photocopy these pages – this will give you enough images to produce one bauble for each design.

2 The baubles are available from most craft shops and come with a flat centre section and a dome that can be fitted on to just one side or on both, making a round bauble. If you photocopy the illustrations twice you can place the pictures back to back, on either side of the centre section and produce a spherical bauble.

3 The six copies of the designs are cut up into layers to allow the background to recede and the items in the foreground to become more prominent. Cut around one complete design to form the base layer. This is glued on to one side of the flat plastic centre of the bauble using spray adhesive or double-sided sticky tape. The subsequent layers are cut using small scissors or a craft knife and cutting mat, then attached using blobs of silicone glue.

Making the robin design

1 From the six photocopies of the robin design, cut one complete picture and fix it in place on the flat plastic centre of the bauble

using spray adhesive or double-sided sticky tape: this is the base layer.

2 For the second layer, cut out the robin, trees and fields, leaving off just the sky area. Apply tiny blobs of silicone randomly over the robin and snow covered scenery on the base layer. Carefully position the second layer on to the blobs using tweezers: do not press on the paper or the silicone may spread and be seen from the front of the picture. Use a cocktail stick to nudge the image into position, lining up the tree tops and outline of the robin.

3 For the third layer, cut out the robin, leaf and fence post, removing the small area of sky between his beak. Fix in place as before using silicone blobs. The fourth layer is the robin, leaf and snow on the top of the fence post, leaving off the fence post.

4 For the top layer, cut out the robin's wing, head and leaf. Using scissors, make long cuts between each wing feather. In between these cuts, make smaller cuts around the edge of each feather: hold the scissors in one hand and the robin in the other, turn your wrists inward, tilting the heels of both thumbs downward and towards each other. This will

lay the scissor blades at an acute angle almost touching the paper. The cut paper will curl slightly producing feathers: the finer the cuts, the more realistic the feathers will look (see Furring and Feathering, page 9). Fix in place as before using silicone blobs. Press the dome in place over the robin.

Making the teddy design

1 Place the complete base layer of the teddy picture in place using spray adhesive. The second layer is cut in two pieces: the armchair, and the table, tree and presents. Fix in place on to the base layer using silicone blobs. Cut the third layer in three pieces: the tree, the two parcels at the front, and the teddy, arms and front of the chair. The final layer is in five pieces: the pink present, teddy's foot pads, his muzzle and bow tie; fix in place using silicone.

Making the village scene

1 Fix the complete base layer in place. Cut away the sky for the second layer. On the third layer cut away the sky and the church, leaving the lych gate and fir tree in the centre. Cut the fourth layer in pieces: the cottages on the left and right, and the boy with the sleigh. Fix in place as before and press on the dome.

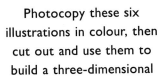

Photocopy these six
illustrations in colour, then
cut out and use them to
build a three-dimensional
robin bauble.

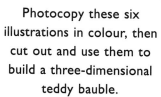

Photocopy these six
illustrations in colour, then
cut out and use them to
build a three-dimensional
teddy bauble.

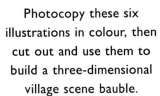

Photocopy these six
illustrations in colour, then
cut out and use them to
build a three-dimensional
village scene bauble.

Stamped Greetings

Stamping is one of the easiest ways of producing the multiple images needed for 3-D découpage. The images can be stamped using black or coloured ink, or they can be embossed giving them a stronger outline. Choose stamps with good clear images and plenty of space between the outlines for adding colour

You will need

- Greetings card blank
- Thick paper
- Wooden plant tag – chopstick
- Napkin ring
- Gift box
- Rubber stamps
- Ink stamp pad
- Stamping ink – black
- Embossing stamp pad
- Embossing ink
- Embossing powder – bronze
- Small scissors, craft knife
- Cutting mat, tweezers, paintbrush
- Acrylic paint – pink, blue
- Varnish – clear matt, glitter glue
- Silicone glue or double-sided fixing tabs
- Felt-tipped pens – yellow, red, blue, green, orange, brown, black, pink
- Small spice seeds, PVA glue or spray adhesive

Making a stamped image

1 To make a 3-D picture choose stamps similar to those used for this project. Spread the ink pad with stamping ink and allow it to soak well into the pad before using.

2 Take your chosen stamp and press on to the ink pad; remove from the pad and stamp it on to thick paper or thin card, before lifting carefully off. You may want to practise applying the stamp until you achieve an even application. You will need approximately six copies of the image.

3 Allow the ink to dry and then colour the image with felt-tipped pens before cutting out the design, following the instructions on page 28. Wash the stamp in warm soapy water to remove the excess ink, and dry completely.

Making an embossed image

1 Spread embossing ink on to a clean stamp pad and allow to soak in thoroughly.

2 Press the stamp on to the pad and then on to thick paper or thin card. Before the ink dries, sprinkle embossing powder over the stamped design; leave for a few seconds then tap off the excess powder, returning it to the pot. Practise the process several times on a spare piece of paper until you can achieve a good clean image.

3 To emboss the ink: hold the card over a toaster or cooker hob for a few seconds until the powder bubbles, but do not overheat the embossing powder or it will lose its shine. Allow to dry then colour the image.

Colouring the stamp

1 Look at the stamped design and decide which areas are in the background, which are in the foreground and which are in between.

2 The upper layers of the picture will need more detailed colouring than the lower layers. It will also be necessary to colour the cut edges of the paper pieces, or they will show as white in the picture (see Finishing Techniques, page 12). With some of the smaller pieces it may be easier to colour the design before cutting it out.

Applying the layers

1 Having planned your design carefully, cut out a base layer, using scissors; for the smaller pieces you may find it easier to use a sharp craft knife and cutting mat. Stick this layer flat on to your chosen surface using PVA glue or spray mount.

2 Colour and cut a second layer in the same way, and fix exactly over the base layer: use the end of a cocktail stick to apply 5mm (1/4in) blobs of silicone to the base layer. Position the paper piece on to the silicone blobs using tweezers; do not press the paper down or the silicone will spread and may show in the picture. Use a cocktail stick to nudge the paper piece into position; try to get the piece exactly over the shape underneath (see Building a Picture, page 10). Continue adding layers in the same way, applying the silicone to the base and not to the back of the paper pieces, while taking care to keep the silicone away from the edges of the design.

Making the card

1 Stamp and emboss six copies of a house design. Colour the images as before.

2 Cut out and fix the base layer centrally on to the front of a greetings card using PVA glue or spray adhesive. Add a second layer as before using silicone blobs.

3 For the third layer, cut out the house, removing the house wall, but leaving the windows, roof, door, steps and railings. Fix in place using silicone. For the fourth layer cut as before, then remove the roof, window panes and door: this leaves the window frames, window boxes, door pillars, steps and railings.

4 The fifth layer consists of just the shutters, door pillars, steps and railings, and the final layer is the front step and railings. Decorate the edge of the card with a line of glitter glue.

Making a plant tag

1 Cut a rectangle of card slightly larger than your stamped image or the part of the image that you are using; glue a wooden chopstick to the back using PVA glue. Paint with two coats of pink acrylic paint and one coat of matt varnish, leaving to dry between coats.

2 Stamp or emboss a floral butterfly design six times on to paper or card, then colour with felt-tipped pens.

3 Cut out the base layer carefully and fix on to the plant tag with PVA glue or spray adhesive. Cut more layers, leaving off some parts of the design as you work forward with the layers; the butterfly should be the final layer.

Making the napkin ring

1 Paint a wooden napkin ring with two coats of blue acrylic paint, allow to dry then apply a coat of clear matt varnish.

2 Choose a small design or part of a design similar to the sunflowers in the picture to decorate the napkin ring. Stamp or emboss four copies of the design as before.

3 Colour the design then cut out and apply the base layer to the napkin ring using PVA glue or spray adhesive, then allow to dry. Apply more layers using silicone glue, cutting

away parts of the design as you move forward with the layers.

4 For a floral design you can add extra interest to the final layer using spice seeds; paint the seeds black then glue them on to the centre of the flower using PVA glue.

5 As the napkin ring will be subjected to heavy use, for extra protection seal the design with a coat of clear matt varnish or clear nail polish (see Finishing Techniques, page 12).

Decorating the gift box

1 Paint a small gift box with two coats of yellow acrylic paint, and the lid with blue, then finish with a coat of matt varnish, leaving to dry between coats.

2 Choose a design that will fit the box top. Stamp or emboss the design six times then colour using felt-tipped pens. Cut more layers, removing parts of the design as you move forward with the layers; fix the layers as before.

Jungle Lamp and Picture

Make this wildlife lamp and picture from scraps of wallpaper left over
when decorating a child's bedroom. The lamp base is made from a cookie
jar, which has been fitted with a lampholder and flex. To complete the
look add a decorated shade and wildlife picture using similar motifs

You will need

- Wallpaper or border with a wildlife theme
- Lampshade
- Glass storage jar with cork lid
- Green tissue paper
- Lampholder and flex – purchase ready
  assembled from an electrical supplier
- Frame with deep recess
- Handmade paper
- Small scissors, craft knife
- Cutting mat, tweezers
- Silicone glue
- PVA glue

Cutting and assembling

1 Choose a wallpaper or border where the
animal images stand out well against the
jungle. If a leaf or bush is covering part of an
animal, this can be cut out and included in the
design. For special cutting techniques, see
Furring and Feathering on page 9.

2 The animals should have about 5 or 6
layers, or part layers. For the elephant: cut
out the complete image for the base layer and
stick in position using PVA glue; cut out the
same image for the second layer and attach over
the first using silicone blobs; for the third cut
the bush on the right, and attach to the bush
on the previous layer. For the fourth layer cut
the head, ears, trunk and palm leaves, and again
use silicone to position. The fifth layer is split
into two parts: the palm leaves on the left, and
the elephant's face and trunk, not including his
ears. Position the leaves on the silicone,
overlapping the elephant's ear; the face is
attached in the same way. Cut out and position
the left tusk to finish. Place another elephant in
a recessed frame, following the instructions for
the Botanical Picture on page 14.

3 Overlap the animals, building up a jungle
scene on the front of a glass jar. Fill the
completed jar with crumpled tissue, then fix an
electrical fitting to the top, before adding a
shade, decorated with animals.

Victorian Fashion Plate

This fashion plate has been cleverly adapted into a three-dimensional picture, from a design in a turn of the century Parisian fashion magazine. Plates like these were used to show women the very latest dress styles, which they could make at home, or have made for them by a seamstress

You will need

- Wooden box frame to fit the design
- Colour photocopy of pages 34, 35, 36 and 37
- Stiff card
- Mounting board – cream
- Craft knife, cutting mat, scissors
- Silicone glue
- Cocktail stick
- Self-adhesive sticky pads
- Spray adhesive

Preparing the frame

1 Cut a rectangle of stiff card to fit into the frame: the base layer of your picture will be fixed to this. Cut a mount from cream card that will fit around the picture, just overlapping the base layer: the mount opening should be no larger than 12.5x17.5cm (5x6¾in) or the edges of the base layer will not be hidden.

Copying the design

1 On pages 34–37 you will find all the parts needed to assemble the picture. Colour photocopy each page on to good quality copier paper.

2 The parts have been labelled to make assembling the picture easier; as the labels will be detached when the pieces are cut out, it will help to write the label information lightly on to the back of the pieces using a pencil.

3 Using a craft knife and cutting mat or small sharp scissors carefully cut out each piece of the picture. Sort the pieces into their respective areas: including the base layer, the lady has five layers; the pink hollyhock five layers, and the other hollyhocks have three layers. The last three layers of the pink hollyhock; the final layer of the hollyhocks around the border; and two layers of the lady's gown should be fixed above the mount.

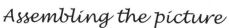

Assembling the picture

1 Using spray adhesive, fix the base layer centrally on to the backing card: always use spray adhesive in a well ventilated room, and cover your work surface with newspaper.

2 All the layers are applied using blobs of silicone glue 2mm (¹/₁₆in) high on to the fixed layer, not to the back of the paper piece being attached. Keep the silicone well away from the edges of the paper, and avoid getting it on your fingers, or it may mark the paper.

3 Use tweezers to position the pieces on to the silicone, and a cocktail stick to nudge them gently into position. Make sure that each piece is directly over the picture beneath: this is important as the overall effect will be spoilt if the layers are not exactly in line.

4 Position the second layer of the central blue hollyhock on to the base layer using silicone blobs. Next the second layer of the lady, with her hand over the hollyhock, and a second layer of all the other hollyhocks.

5 On the back of the mounting board fix a double layer of the self-adhesive sticky pads, in the corners and down each side of the mount. Line up the cut-out area of the mount over the base picture and press in place.

6 Add the third layer of the lady, taking the bottom of her dress over the mount. Fix the final layers of the pink hollyhocks, taking the top of the flower on the third layer over the mount. Finish the other flowers in the same way, taking the smaller hollyhock flowers at the edges over the mount.

7 Position the frame centrally over the picture, then attach the backing board to the frame using tape.

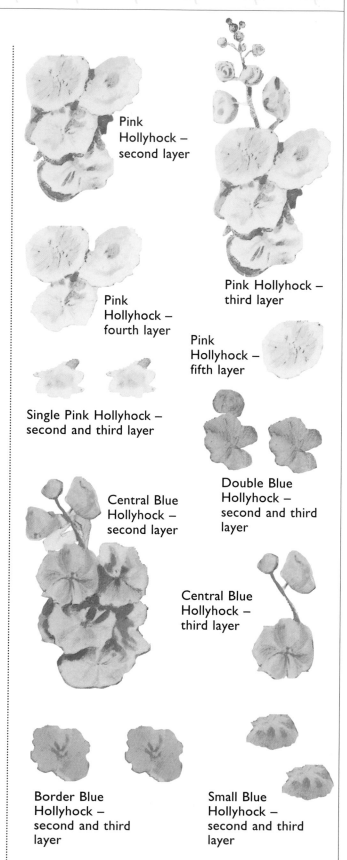

Pink Hollyhock – second layer

Pink Hollyhock – third layer

Pink Hollyhock – fourth layer

Pink Hollyhock – fifth layer

Single Pink Hollyhock – second and third layer

Double Blue Hollyhock – second and third layer

Central Blue Hollyhock – second layer

Central Blue Hollyhock – third layer

Border Blue Hollyhock – second and third layer

Small Blue Hollyhock – second and third layer

Complete Picture –
base layer

Cut out around the outer edges
of all the pieces and use them to
build a three dimensional picture.

Lady – second layer

Lady – fifth layer

Mauve Hollyhocks –
second and third layers

36

Cut out around the outer edges
of all the pieces and use them to
build a three dimensional picture.

Lady – fourth layer

Lady – third layer

Hat – fourth and
fifth layers

Nativity Picture and Card

This nativity scene made from coloured paper is sure to become a favourite decoration that will be brought out every Christmas, along with the tinsel and baubles. Any part of the design can be made into a card; or if you prefer, extend the scene by removing the arch and adding palm trees and a camel

If you would like to change the size of the nativity scene or card, use a photocopier to enlarge or reduce the templates on pages 40-41.

You will need

- Wooden box frame – 17x12cm (6¾x4⅞in)
- Greetings card blank 18x11cm (7x4½in) – blue
- Craft paper – blue, white, gold, beige, brown
- Acrylic paint – gold
- White paper, pencil
- Spray adhesive
- Silicone glue
- Double-sided sticky tape
- Craft knife, cutting mat, scissors

Preparing the box

1 Paint the sides of a box frame with two coats of gold acrylic paint, then leave to dry.

Cutting the background

1 Cut a piece of blue paper to fit the back of the picture, then attach to the back using spray adhesive: always use spray adhesive in a well ventilated room.

2 Make a tracing of the arch on page 41 on to white paper. Lay the template on to white craft paper, and draw around with a pencil; cut out the arch. Apply blobs of silicone glue to the blue paper, then position the arch on the silicone. Cut the floor strip from beige paper and the star from gold; use silicone blobs to space them away from the background.

Assembling the picture

1 Trace over the templates on pages 40 and 41 using white paper; cut out the shapes. Lay the templates on to card, following the photograph for colour, and draw around with a pencil; cut out carefully.

2 Attach the front straw behind the front manger, using double-sided tape; repeat for the back, matching the dotted lines to the upper edges of the mangers. When dry, fold the straw over. Using silicone blobs, attach the manger back to the background, and the baby's

body, head and halo to the back manger. Finally attach the front manger over the top.

3 Use silicone to attach Mary and Joseph's body and head to the background, adding Joseph's beard, the headdresses and headbands.

4 Attach the first king's body to the background using silicone, positioning him slightly in front of Mary, Joseph and the manger. Use silicone to attach the casket, head and hand before the cloak, beard and the headdress.

5 Fix the second king's body and head in place on the same level as the first king, using silicone. Add the casket, hand and arm, and finally the headdress, band and beard.

6 Fix the third king's body and head in place using larger blobs of silicone, bringing him slightly more forward than the other two and overlapping the second king; attach the headdress and jewel.

7 Using a sharp craft knife and cutting board, cut spirals on the sheep's body. Attach the sheep over the bottom of the first king's body, with the sheep's head and fringe on top.

Making the Christmas card

1 Trace over the templates opposite for the card. Lay the templates on to card, following the photograph for colour, and draw around the edges. Cut out then attach using silicone glue.

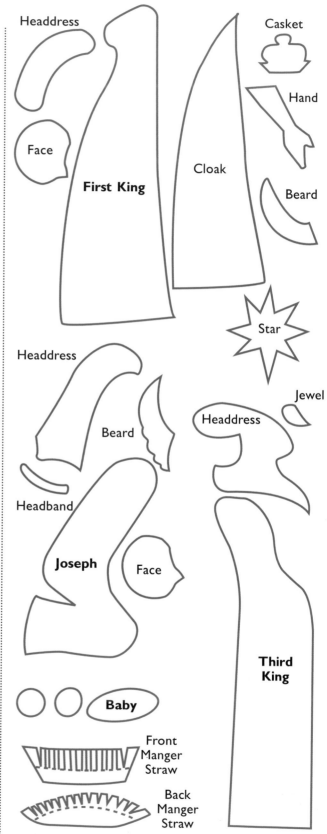

Headdress

Casket

Face

Hand

First King

Cloak

Beard

Star

Headdress

Jewel

Headdress

Beard

Headband

Joseph

Face

Third King

Baby

Front Manger Straw

Back Manger Straw

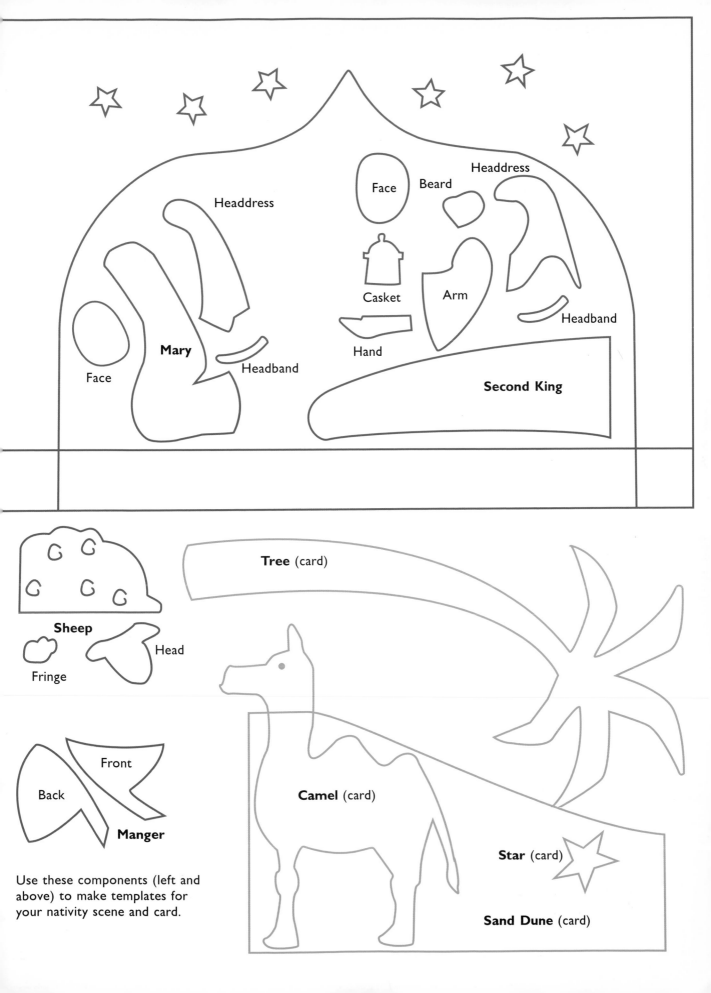

Headdress

Face Beard Headdress

Mary

Casket Arm

Face Hand

Headband

Headband

Second King

Sheep

Tree (card)

Fringe Head

Front

Back

Manger

Camel (card)

Star (card)

Use these components (left and above) to make templates for your nativity scene and card.

Sand Dune (card)

Circus Fun Desk Set

This fun desk set, suitable for a child's room, is easy to make from card and crinkle card. Some elements of the design are mounted directly on to the background, while others are layered using self-adhesive sticky pads. The clowns have also been mounted on to a box file and pen holder

You will need

- Assorted crinkle card – yellow, red, blue, white, gold, pink
- Assorted thin card – yellow, deep blue, dark grey, peach, blue, pink, red, pale blue, white, green
- Stiff cardboard – 30x25cm (12x10in)
- Picture frame – 30x25cm (12x10in)
- Cardboard pot
- Empty cereal box
- Craft knife, cutting mat, small scissors
- Typewriter carbon paper, white paper
- Felt-tipped pens, pencil, ruler, ball-point pen
- Double-sided self-adhesive sticky pads
- PVA glue, spray paint – red
- Tweezers, cocktail stick
- Star-shaped punch, black cotton

Making the background

1 Cut a piece of stiff backing board to fit into the frame. Using scissors, cut a piece of green card to fit the lower two thirds of the picture, making the top edge uneven for the hills. Cut a piece of pale blue card to fit the sky area, extending the bottom edge so that it will fit down behind the hills. Glue the sky and hills on to the backing using PVA glue.

Making the templates

1 Make tracings of the templates on pages 46-47 using white paper.

2 On some of the templates, like the clouds, it will be possible to cut out the tracing, lay it on the card and draw around the outside edge.

3 For the more detailed shapes, lay carbon paper on top of the card, ink side down, then over this lay the tracing. Carefully go over the lines with a ball-point pen. This will leave a line on the card which can be cut out using either a craft knife or small scissors.

Making trees and clouds

1 Make tracings of the trees, clouds and sun. From white crinkle card cut the clouds; use yellow for the sun and gold for the trees. Arrange on the background, overlapping the green and blue card, then glue in position using PVA glue.

2 Make a template of the tent. Cut some parts from the red crinkle card and some from the white, using the photograph above as a guide; the flag is cut from dark blue crinkle card. Glue on to the background using PVA glue.

Making the vehicles

1 Make tracings of the lorry and trailer. From dark blue crinkle card cut out the lorry. Using a star punch make a selection of stars from yellow, white and pink crinkle card. Glue the stars on to the lorry, and then the lorry on to the background. Cut out circles from yellow crinkle card for the lorry wheels, and glue them in position on the lorry. Cut the trailer from pink crinkle card and the wheels from blue. Do not fix the trailer in place at this stage of the project.

Making the ringmaster

1 Make tracings of the ringmaster parts, then cut his shirt from red card. Use a black felt-tipped pen to add a collar, buttons and cuff.

Cut two face shapes from peach card, and two hats from grey; add detail to one face and one hat using felt-tipped pens. Glue the ringmaster's shirt inside the window opening of the lorry; on to this glue one unmarked head, and a hat slightly overlapping the face. Cut self-adhesive sticky pads into small pieces, peel off the backing paper, and attach them to the centre of the face and hat using tweezers. Position the decorated face and hat on to the pads, making sure they are exactly over the shapes beneath. Cut out one hand from peach card and glue it under the end of the sleeve.

Making the small clown

1 Cut two body shapes for the small clown from pink card. On one shape add spots and stripes using felt-tipped pens.

2 Cut two faces and four hands from peach card; add the features to one face using felt-tipped pens. Cut out two hat shapes and four shoes from bright blue card.

3 Stick the undecorated clown's body, feet, hands, face and hat on to the background using PVA glue, slightly overlapping the pieces. Cover the clown with small pieces of self-adhesive sticky pad, then carefully position the decorated pieces on top, making sure that they are directly over the pieces beneath. Add small circles of silver paper to the clown's hat, and glue hair made from short lengths of yellow crinkle card either side of the face.

4 Cut out three balloons from crinkle card and three short lengths of black cotton. Use a cocktail stick to press the cotton on to tiny blobs of PVA glue, then glue the balloons to the end of the cotton.

Making the large clown

1 Cut out two coats and four shoes from blue card; two pairs of trousers from pink card, two hats from yellow card; two faces and four hands from peach card, and hair from red crinkle card. Decorate one set of parts with felt-tipped pens.

2 Use PVA glue to attach the base layer, and pieces of self-adhesive sticky pad to attach the decorated layer over the base. Add three balloons in the same way as for the small clown.

Making the elephant

1 Cut the elephant's body pieces, head and ear from dark grey card; the blanket and headdress from pink card; and from white card, four small squares for the elephant's toenails, two small triangles for his eyes, and two triangles for his tusks. With felt-tipped pens add shading to the ear and trunk. Use PVA glue to attach the base layer, and pieces of self-adhesive sticky pad to attach the second layer, adding the blanket with glue. Use the sticky pads to attach the head, adding the eyes and tusks with glue, then attach the ear on sticky pads.

Making the lion

1 Cut the lion pieces from yellow card, adding detail to the mane and body using felt-tipped pens.

2 Using sticky pads attach the mane and face to the lion's body. Weave the lion's body through the bars of the trailer, leaving his head protruding out. Fix the lion and the trailer behind the lorry, adding two circles of blue crinkle card for the wheels.

Making the seals

1 From dark grey card cut out the seals' body parts, flipping the templates for the second seal; add shading with a black felt-tipped pen. Glue the base layer with PVA, then add the body and flippers on sticky pads. From the yellow and red crinkle card cut out a ball shape. Glue the ball above one seal on the background. Use small pieces of black cotton for the seals' whiskers.

Making the grass

1 Cut spiky tufts of grass from gold crinkle card and glue along the front edge of the picture. Decorate with small flower shapes cut from pink and yellow crinkle card.

Making the box and pen pot

1 Cut the top from a cereal box, then cut away the sides at an angle. Glue pale green card on to the inside surface of the box, and yellow crinkle card on the outside. Punch stars from coloured card and glue them around the edge of the box. Enlarge the clown trace on a photocopier to fit the box. Cut out the pieces, then attach to the side of the box, making up in the same way as for the picture.

2 Spray or paint a cardboard pot inside and out with red paint. Attach a large and small clown to the side of the pot.

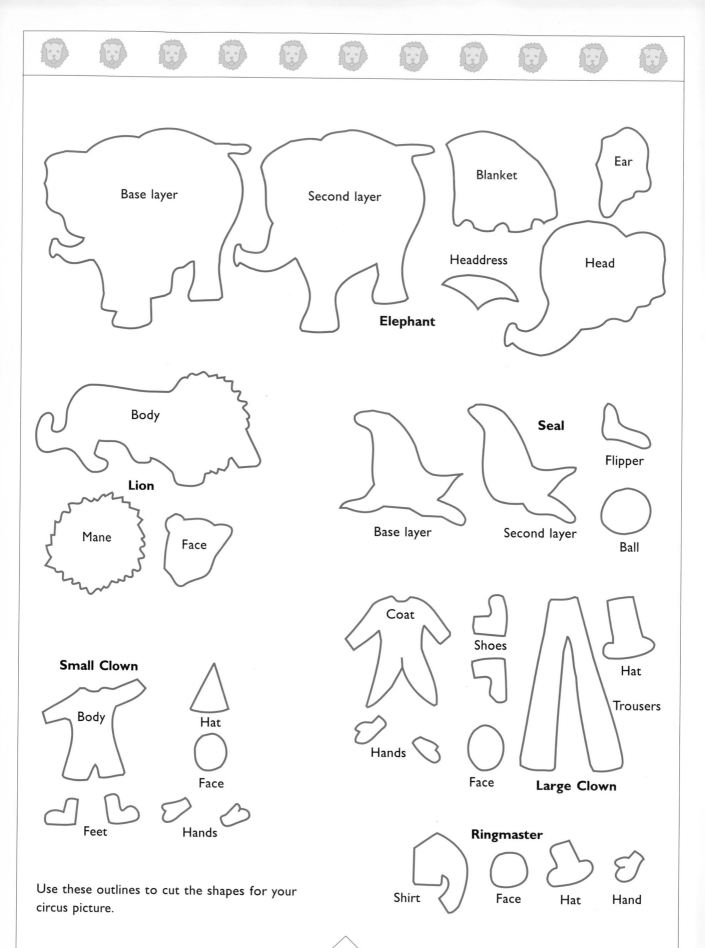

Base layer

Second layer

Blanket

Ear

Headdress

Head

Elephant

Body

Lion

Seal

Flipper

Mane

Face

Base layer

Second layer

Ball

Coat

Shoes

Hat

Small Clown

Hat

Body

Trousers

Face

Hands

Feet

Hands

Face

Large Clown

Ringmaster

Use these outlines to cut the shapes for your circus picture.

Shirt

Face

Hat

Hand

Strawberry Gift Holders

These pretty gift holders are a must for summer celebrations; each one is made using a strawberry motif, cut from lightweight furnishing fabric. The fabric is then mounted on to a bag, box or teapot-shaped gift holder using self-adhesive sticky pads

You will need

- Lightweight furnishing fabric with a repeat pattern
- Lightweight furnishing fabric 25x20cm (10x7in) – blue
- Medium weight iron-on interfacing
- Card 25x20cm (10x7in) – blue
- Gift bag – blue
- Gift box – white
- Self-adhesive sticky pads
- White paper, pencil
- White tacky fabric/paper glue
- Glitter glue – red
- Narrow ribbon – red
- Scissors

Choosing the fabric

1 As you will need at least three layers to make the images look three-dimensional, choose a floral fruit fabric with a close pattern repeated. The material should be a lightweight furnishing fabric with a tight weave.

Making the gift bag

1 From the fabric choose a group of flowers or fruit that will fit the paper gift bag, then cut around the edge, leaving a border of 2cm (1in). Iron medium weight interfacing on to the back of the fabric, then trim off the surplus with small scissors. This will prevent the fabric from fraying when cut, and add stiffness to the design.

2 Fix the base layer on to the side of the gift bag using white tacky glue; leave to dry.

3 Cut out a second layer exactly the same shape as the first. Cut up self-adhesive sticky pads into small pieces, peel off the backing paper on both sides, and stick on to the base fabric. You will need to position the pads close enough together to hold up the fabric without sagging: the closeness of the pads will depend on the thickness of the material you are using.

4 For the third layer cut out the parts of the design that are furthest forward: on this

fabric these are the two large strawberries at the front of the group, and a smaller strawberry at the top. Fix in place using small pieces of self-adhesive sticky pad.

Making the gift box

1 Choose fabric motifs that will fit on to the sides of the gift box. Iron interfacing on to the back of the fabric, and cut out the design. The base layer should be stuck in place using white tacky glue; allow to dry.

2 For the second layer cut out the parts of the design that are furthest forward. Attach to the base using self-adhesive sticky pads.

Making the teapot shape

1 Draw over the teapot design opposite and make a tracing on to white paper. Cut out the shape, including the tabs.

2 Cut a piece of blue fabric and interfacing, just larger than the template. Iron the interfacing on to the back of the fabric with a warm iron. Glue thin blue card on to the interfacing on the back of the fabric using white tacky glue; leave to dry. Lay the template of the teapot on to the card side of the blue fabric; draw around the outside and cut out.

3 Fold one tab, along the dotted lines shown on the teapot outline opposite; bend the outer section of the tab inward, and glue to the inside of the teapot; at the other end of the tab, fold inward on the edge of the teapot, then push the tab in at the centre, making a concertina fold. Repeat for the other tab, then make similar creases on the base, folding along the bottom edge of both teapot halves, making a flat area on to which the teapot can stand.

Cutting the fabric

1 Choose fabric motifs that will fit on to the front of the teapot. Iron interfacing on to the back of the fabric, and cut out several layers of the design. The base layer should be stuck in place using white tacky glue, and the second and third layers positioned using self-adhesive sticky pads. Repeat for the other side of the teapot.

2 Add a line of red glitter glue around the outside edge on both sides of the teapot and along the line of the lid. When the glitter is dry, fill the inside with crumpled tissue paper and tie with a ribbon bow.

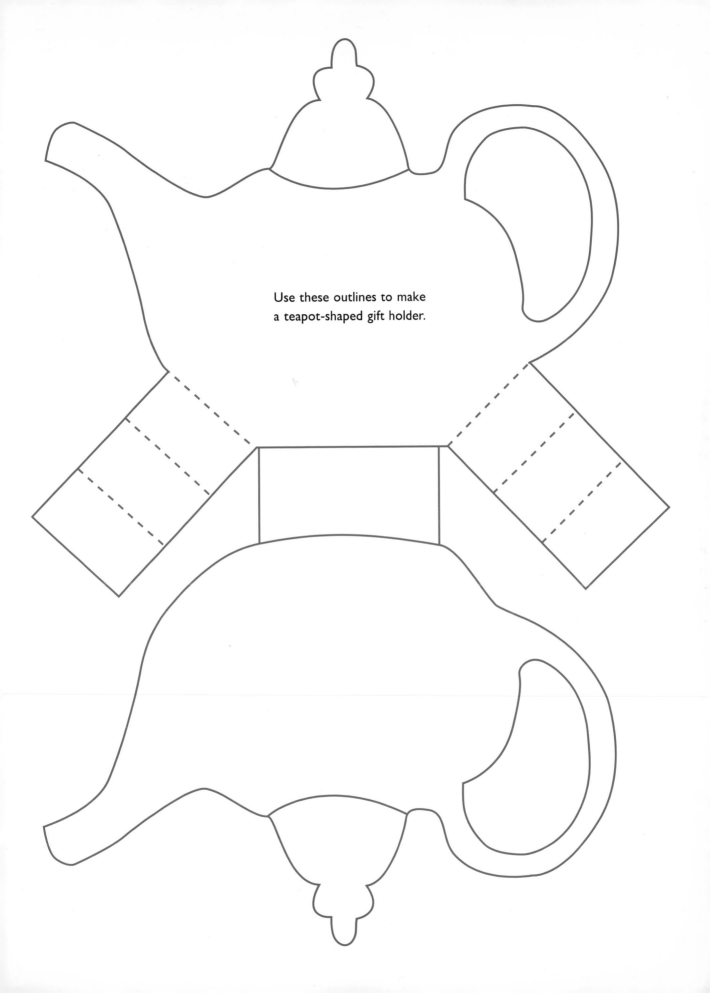

Use these outlines to make
a teapot-shaped gift holder.

Greetings Cards

To build these fun designs, colour photocopy the original drawings given with this project and then layer the parts on to a blank greetings card using tabs. The designs make a great gift for any football enthusiast or train spotter's birthday; and after the celebration's over the cards can be framed and displayed on the wall

These designs can also be worked on cardboard and then mounted into a frame.

You will need

- Greetings card blanks – 197×150cm (6x8in)
- Craft knife, cutting mat, scissors
- Stiff card
- Spray adhesive
- PVA glue, small paintbrush
- Blunt knife
- Newspaper

Copying the design

1 On pages 56 and 57 you will find the illustrations needed to build the footballer and train greetings cards. Colour photocopy the pages on to the stiffest paper that will work in the photocopier. If this is not possible, back the photocopies with thick paper or stiff cardboard using spray adhesive. Always use spray adhesive in a well-ventilated room, and cover your work surface with newspaper.

Cutting out the train card

1 Using scissors, cut out the tunnel around the outer black line: this is the base layer of the design.

2 The small train forms the second layer. Cut out tab A and score along the dotted lines with the back of a blunt knife. Concertina fold both ends of the tab, then glue the centre of the tab on to the back of the train using PVA.

3 Cut out the rail track with the tabs attached: this is the third layer. Score along the dotted lines and bend the tabs back behind the picture. Fold again forming a concertina fold on both tabs.

4 Cut out the large train around the outer black line using scissors, then cut out the centre circle with a craft knife. Cut out the two pieces marked tab B, and score along the

dotted lines, then fold both blue ends down into a 'u' shape. Apply PVA glue to the shaded area on one side of the tab, and fix in place on the back of the large train, 2cm (1in) from the top. Make sure the bridge of the tab is uppermost. Fix the second tab 2cm (1in) up from the bottom of the train, with the bridge of the tab at the bottom.

Assembling the train

1 Measure down 3cm (1¼in) from the top of a greetings card, and mark lightly with a pencil. This is where you will fix the top of the tab on the back of the large train.

2 Make another pencil mark 5cm (2in) down from the top of the card. Lay the tunnel face down on a piece of newspaper; apply a coating of spray adhesive to the back of the shape. Place the tunnel centrally on to the card, lining the top of the tunnel up with the pencil mark.

3 Apply a little PVA glue to the back of the shaded ends of the tab on the small train, then carefully fix the train over the tunnel, with the bottom of the train level with the floor of the tunnel.

4 Apply a little PVA glue to the back of the shaded tabs on the track. Position it over the tunnel, lining up the grass line on the track, and just overlapping the bottom of the small train.

5 On the back of the large train, apply glue to the shaded ends of the upper and lower tabs. Position the train level on the card, lining the upper tab with the pencil mark, and making sure that the small train is central in the cut-out. With the card flat on your work surface, slip your finger between the layers and apply pressure to the ends of the tabs, making sure they are stuck firmly on to the card.

6 When the glue is completely dry the layers can be flattened enabling the card to fit into an envelope.

Cutting out the football card

1 Using scissors, cut out the crowd circle: this is the base layer of the design.

2 The goal forms the second layer; cut out including the tabs, then score along the dotted lines and fold both ends into a concertina shape.

3 Cut out the footballer's leg with the tabs attached. Score along the dotted line as before and bend the tabs back behind the picture; fold again forming a concertina.

4 Cut out the large footballer with scissors, then remove the centre circle with a craft knife. Cut out the two tabs marked B and score along the dotted lines, then fold both ends of each tab down into a 'u' shape. Apply PVA to the shaded areas on the tabs, then fix one tab in place on the back of the footballer's head, with the bridge of the tab uppermost; and the other 2cm (1in) down from the bottom

of the cut-out, with the bridge of the tab facing towards the bottom.

Assembling the football card

1 Measure down 4cm (1½in) from the top of the greetings card, and mark lightly with a pencil: this is where you will fix the top of the tab on the back of the footballer.

2 Make another mark 6cm (2¼in) down from the top of the card. Glue the crowd circle centrally on the card using PVA, lining up the top of the circle with this mark.

3 Apply a little PVA glue to the back of the shaded area of the tabs on the goal, and carefully fix it over the crowd circle, lining up the grass levels.

4 On the footballer's leg, apply glue to the reverse of the shaded area on the tabs, then place at the bottom of the goal layer just covering the edge of the grass.

5 On the back of the large footballer, apply glue to the shaded ends of the upper and lower tabs. Position the footballer level on the card, lining the upper tab with the pencil mark, and making sure the footballer's leg is central in the cut-out.

6 With the card flat on your work surface, slip your finger between the layers and apply pressure to the ends of the tabs making sure they are stuck firmly on to the card.

7 When the glue is completely dry the layers can be flattened enabling the card to fit into an envelope.

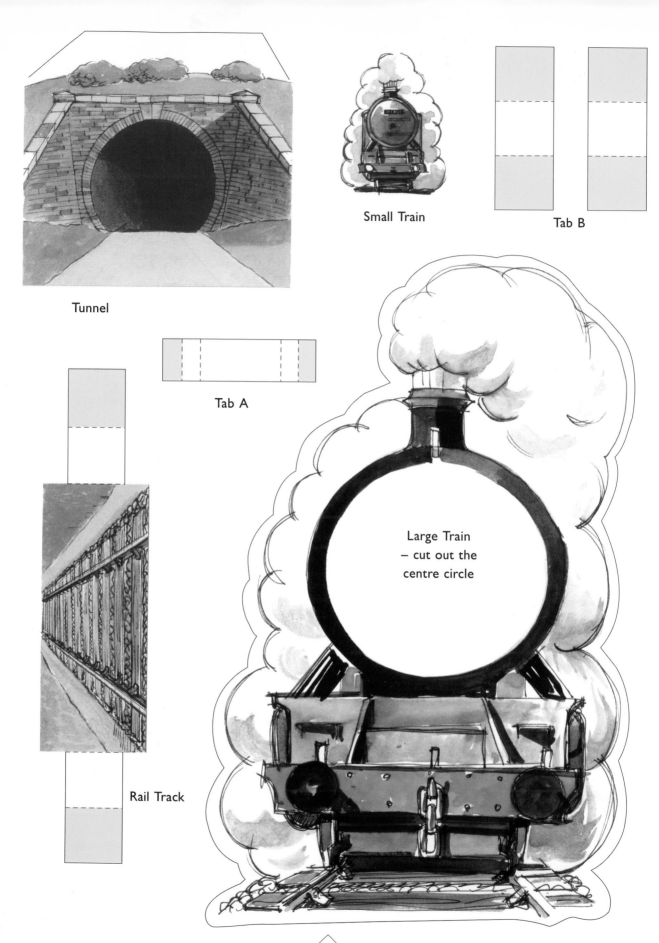

Tunnel

Small Train

Tab B

Tab A

Rail Track

Large Train
– cut out the
centre circle

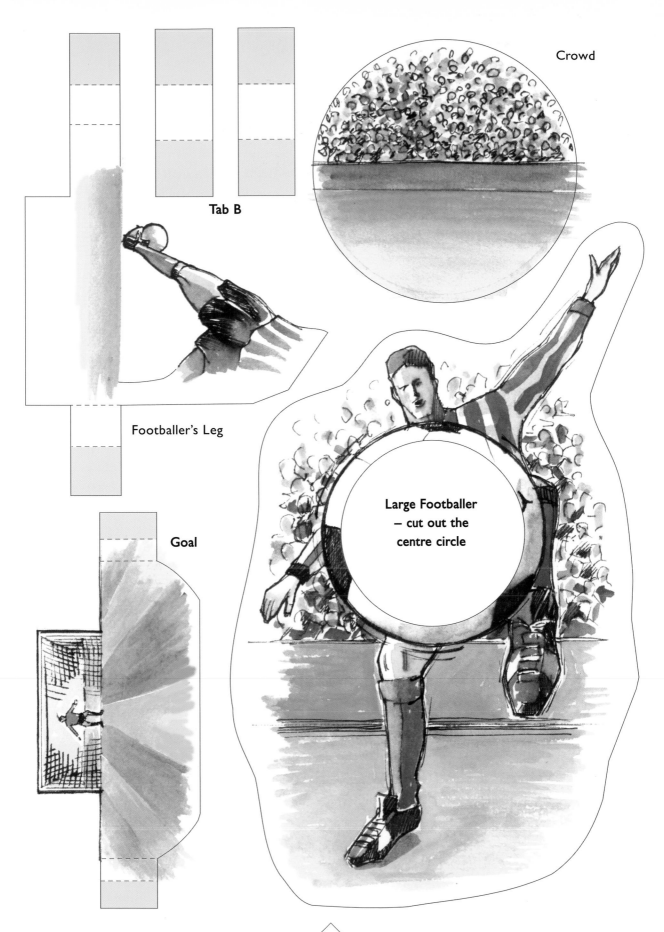

Tab B

Crowd

Footballer's Leg

Goal

Large Footballer
– cut out the
centre circle

Pansy Gift Tags

These realistic looking pansy tags have been hand painted using watercolours; each of the delightful pansies has been built from four layers, which are cut from thin watercolour paper. Once painted the pansies are mounted, using silicone, on to parcel labels

You will need
- Parcel labels – mixed colours
- Thin watercolour paper – white
- Silicone glue
- White paper, pencil
- Watercolour paints and paintbrush
- Felt-tipped pens
- Scissors, craft knife, cutting mat
- PVA glue or spray adhesive

Tracing the pansies

1 Using white paper trace over the pansy templates on page 61. For each pansy you will have to cut four layers: the base layer is the complete flower; the second layer is minus the petal shape at the back of the pansy; the third layer is the front three petals, losing the back left and right petals; and the final layer is the front petal. Next to the templates on page 61 is a guide showing the four shapes you will need to cut.

2 Once you have traced the four parts of the pansy you are making, cut out using scissors or a craft knife and cutting mat. This will give four templates for tracing around.

3 Lay the templates on to the watercolour paper and holding them firmly in position, draw around the outline.

Painting the petals

1 Each layer of the pansy should be painted exactly the same as the one above and below: this is essential as when assembled, the markings need to flow between layers forming a complete three-dimensional flower.

2 Follow the photograph opposite for applying the paint: do not brush the paint across the paper, but let the water in the paint spread it across the image filling the shape. If

the paint spreads further than the outlines this can be removed when the petals are cut out. As the centres of the pansies are a different colour to the petals: paint from the centre to the outside, leaving the central area white. When dry paint the centre, leaving a fine line of white paper to form a halo.

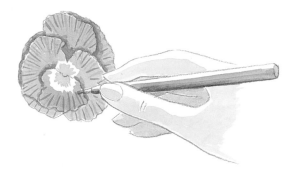

3 Add fine vein markings to the petals using felt-tipped pens.

4 When the painted petals are dry, place the paper on a cutting board, and cut around the edge of each pansy petal, or group of petals, using a sharp craft knife.

5 Using felt-tipped pens or watercolours, colour the cut edges of the petals so that they are a similar in colour to the rest of the flower (see Finishing Techniques, page 12).

Assembling the pansy

1 Attach the base layer of the pansy flat on to a parcel label using PVA glue or spray adhesive. Apply blobs of silicone to the base layer using the end of a cocktail stick: one or two blobs behind each petal should be sufficient, remembering to check the shape of the next layer before adding the blobs, as there will be one petal less. Position the second layer on top of the base using tweezers. Do not push down on the petals, but use a cocktail stick to nudge the piece into position exactly over the petals beneath.

2 Using silicone blobs, fix the third and then the top layer in the same way.

3 Paint a stem and leaves on to each pansy tag, using dark green watercolour paint.

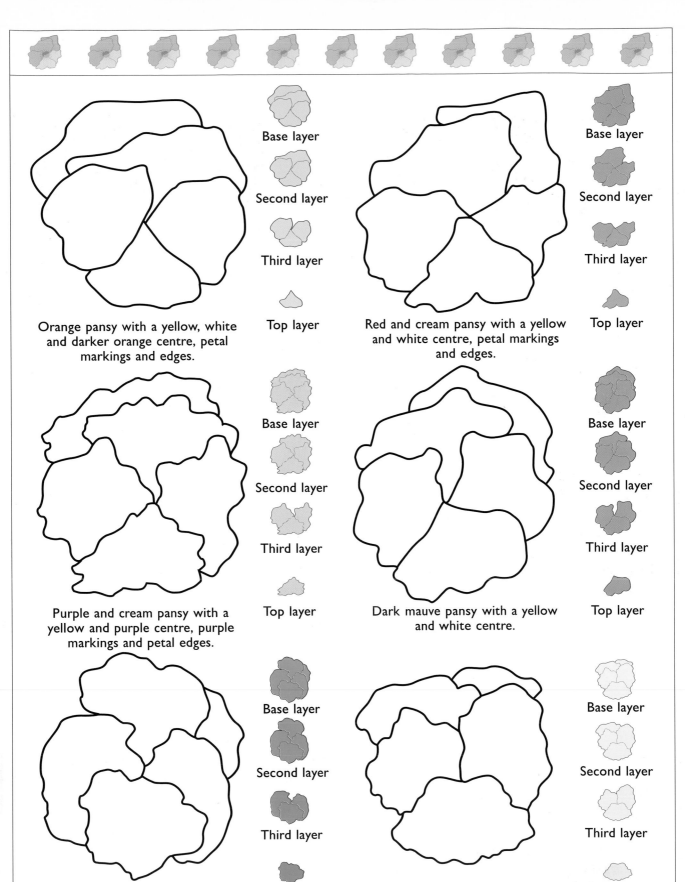

Base layer

Second layer

Third layer

Top layer

Orange pansy with a yellow, white and darker orange centre, petal markings and edges.

Base layer

Second layer

Third layer

Top layer

Red and cream pansy with a yellow and white centre, petal markings and edges.

Base layer

Second layer

Third layer

Top layer

Purple and cream pansy with a yellow and purple centre, purple markings and petal edges.

Base layer

Second layer

Third layer

Top layer

Dark mauve pansy with a yellow and white centre.

Base layer

Second layer

Third layer

Top layer

Lavender or red pansy with yellow and white centres, with mauve or burgundy markings.

Base layer

Second layer

Third layer

Top layer

Yellow pansy with a burgundy and orange centre and orange petal edges.

Acknowledgements

Thanks to the designers for contributing such wonderful projects:
Botanical Picture (page 14), Cheryl Owen
Christmas Baubles (page 20), Fred Fieber and Susan Penny
Stamped Greetings (page 26), Jan Cox and John Underwood
Jungle Lamp and Picture (page 30), Susan Penny
Victorian Fashion Plate (page 32), Jeremy Clements and Susan Penny
Nativity Picture and Card (page 38), Cheryl Owen
Circus Fun Desk Set (page 42), Lynn Strange
Strawberry Gift Holders (page 48), Susan Penny
Greetings Cards (page 52), Fred Fieber
Pansy Gift Tags (page 58), Jan Cox and John Underwood

Thanks to Laura Ashley for allowing us to use their Strawberry fabric for the Gift
Holders project, and their Amazon wallpaper border for the Jungle lamp and picture;
Sutton's for the Heritage wrapping paper used in the Botanical picture; and Funstamps
for the stamps used in the Stamped Greetings project.

Other books in the Made Easy series

Papier Mâché (David & Charles, 1999)

Mosaics (David & Charles, 1999)

Ceramic Painting (David & Charles, 1999)

Stamping (David & Charles, 1998)

Stencilling (David & Charles, 1998)

Glass Painting (David & Charles, 1998)

Silk Painting (David & Charles, 1998)

Suppliers

Craft World (Head office only)
No 8 North Street
Guildford
Surrey GU1 4AF
Tel: 07000 757070
Retail shops nationwide, telephone for local store
(Craft warehouse)

Funstamps Ltd
144 Neilston Road
Paisley
PA2 6QJ
Tel: 0141 884 6441
Telephone for local stockist
(Stamps and stamping equipment)

Hobby Crafts (Head office only)
River Court, Southern Sector
Bournemouth International Airport
Christchurch
Dorset BH23 6SE
Tel: 0800 272387 freephone
Retail shops nationwide, telephone for local store
(Craft warehouse)

Homecrafts Direct
PO Box 38
Leicester LE1 9BU
Tel: 0116 251 3139
Mail order service
(Craft supplies)

Laura Ashley
Customer Services Department
PO Box 19
Newtown
Powys
SY16 1DZ
Tel: 0990 622116
(Furnishing fabric and wallpaper)

Sutton's Consumer Products Ltd
Woodview Road,
Paignton
South Devon
TQ4 7NG
Tel: 0800 7838074 freephone
Telephone for local stockist
(Heritage wrapping paper range)

Index

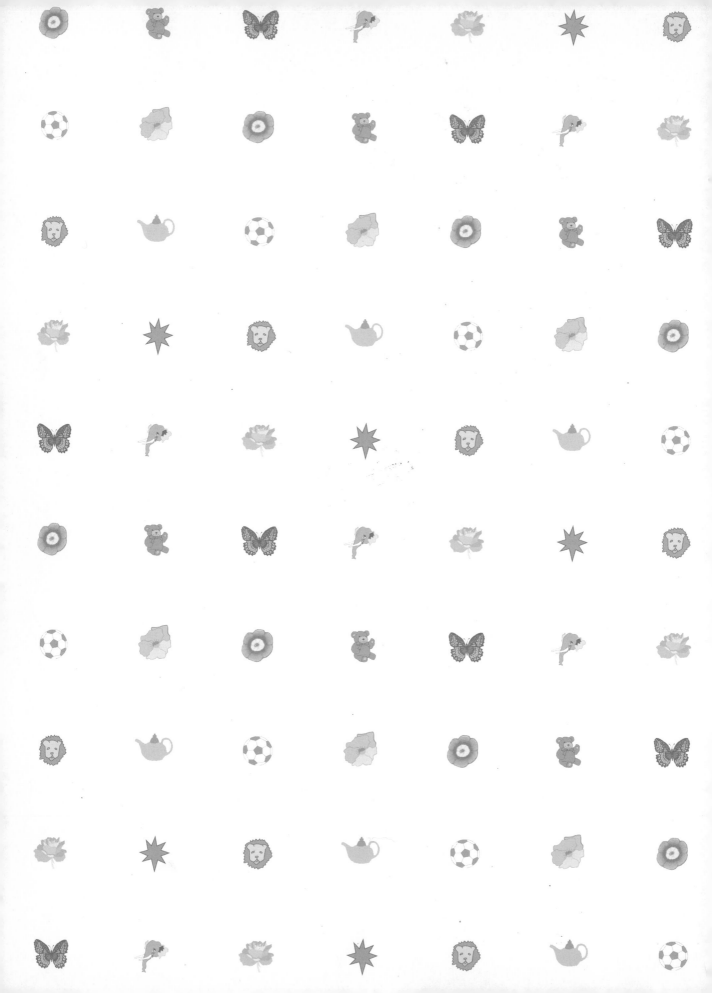